As a hospice social worker, a therapist, and a mom and grandma, I know how important it is to cope with loss. It is one of the most important lessons we can teach our children. It is part of every facet of life. When they learn how to manage when any loss occurs, including the death of someone they love, they can begin to integrate that into their understanding of the cycle of life. More importantly, they will know not to be **afraid** of talking about loss, and about what happens when someone dies.

I wrote this book because children **always** do better with information. What they do not know they will imagine, and many times imagination makes things scary if adults seem stressed or hesitant. Talking with them, answering their questions, and encouraging them to continue to talk about the person who died will allow your children to keep their loved one a part of their lives as they grow up. It's a lesson they will never forget.

I wish you well as you teach your children one of the most important lessons in life, how to cope with loss. May your family's journey through grief end in peace. Jill

Someone I love just died-
What happens now?

Jill A. Johnson-Young, LCSW

Published by Central Counseling Services
6940 Indiana Ave, Suite 275
Riverside CA 92506

www.yourpaththroughgrief.com

© 2018 Jill A. Johnson-Young, LCSW
All rights reserved. No portion of this book may be reproduced in any form without permission from the publisher, except as permitted by U.S. copyright law.
For permissions contact: www.centralcounselingservices.net

Copyright July 2018
Library of Congress Control Number: 2018910729
ISBN: **ISBN-13: 978-0-9997886-2-2**
ISBN-13: 978-1727141764 (CREATESPACE)
ISBN-10: 1727141768

Someone I love just died

Everyone is busy doing stuff, and looking sad

I'm sad too.

I miss them.

The big people are talking about funerals and music and flowers.

People I don't even know are dropping off cookies and food. They tell me to be strong.

They all seem to want to hug me or kiss me or something – I don't even know them!

I'm supposed to not make noise so they can make "*arrangements*" - and make about a million phone calls.

They are making plans. There is going to be a "*viewing*" and a "*funeral*" and then we all go to the *cemetery*.

Some of them seem upset, or mad, or something. They should be getting along, shouldn't they?

I wish I could help.

I don't know what I'm supposed to do or how to act. I wish they would all go away.

I feel all jumbled up inside. I don't want to bother anyone- they're upset, too.

Somebody told me God needed another angel. If He did then he could decide to take someone else.

You know what else?

They aren't in a better place.

It would be better if they were here, with me. It would be better because then none of this would be happening.

They would not be dead.

I'm going to miss my team's practice today. Nobody has time to take me. I really wanted to see my friends.

Some of my friends had someone die. They would understand me more than other people- and my friends wouldn't make me keep talking about this.

I missed practice.

My sister missed gymnastics.

My brother missed swimming.

My brother and sister are acting *weird*. My sister cries and looks sad sometimes. My brother is playing lots of video games because nobody notices how much time he is spending on them.

We're going to go buy suits for the boys and a dress for my sister. She doesn't even like dresses!

When we asked why, they said we would be "*pallbearers*" at the funeral. That's why we had to dress up.

Our job is to walk out of the funeral with the casket. Someone said they would show us how. (It also means lots of people are going to look at us).

On the night of the "*visitation*" we all went to the *mortuary*. Some people call it a *funeral home*. The doors were open and there was a casket in the front, with lots of flowers.

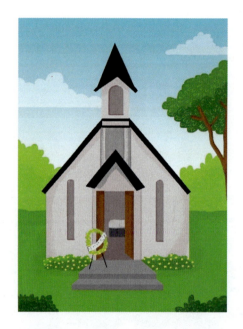

My friend said their family had one for their grandma at their church. Another friend said they did not even have one.

There was a little book to write our names in, and people were talking or whispering.

My brother walked right up to the casket and looked in. My sister didn't want to, so she stayed in the back with our aunt.

I stayed in the back for a while, then walked to the front.

The casket was silver, with shiny handles. It was white inside, with soft fabric. The person I loved was inside, laying down with their head on a pillow.

I thought I might be scared. But it wasn't scary. They were just there.

After lots of people came we went home. We got ice cream on the way. Our parents said we deserved it after such a long evening.

The next morning, we got up and got dressed in our new clothes after breakfast. Someone brought donuts with sprinkles! The grown-ups were trying to be cheerful, but I could see they were a little sad.

We went back to the mortuary, and someone in a dark suit gave us gloves to wear and pinned flowers on us.

My sister was put in charge of people signing the little book from last night.

They had all of us line up around the silver casket before anyone got there and showed us how to help take it out after the funeral was over.

They told us we would help at the cemetery- except some of us weren't tall enough. Our job was to walk with them.

There was music playing, and we sat in front. I guess I did not realize how many people I have in my family. We took up a lot of spaces.

I looked at the casket so I didn't have to see everyone behind us looking at us.

There were prayers, someone talked about the person who died, and more people said nice things about them. One of them was really funny!

We sang some songs, and then the people in the dark suits came up and closed the casket. They told us to come up front.

We stood where they pointed and walked out past *everyone* with the casket. I watched to make sure the flowers didn't fall off.

Then they put the casket in a car that opened in the back, and it slid in on a big tray thing.

Some of the people got in a big car all together. I got in our car with my parents and we drove to the cemetery in a big line called a *procession*. There were people on motorcycles to make sure we stayed together.

When we got there the people in the dark suits were already there, and there was a big tent like you take to the beach covering a place to sit.

We lined up at the car where we put the casket at the mortuary. It's called a *hearse*. The dark suit people opened the door and helped everyone pull it out.

We walked it to the silver stand. Over the hole in the ground. We made sure it was not going to fall. I was peeking underneath to see how it worked.

I could see my mom using her eyes to tell me not to get too close.

Then everyone sat down on the folding chairs. I stood on the side with the other kids. We heard more prayers, and some more words, and then it was over. It felt a little weird to be leaving the casket behind on the stand. They told us it was okay, and the people would stay and make sure everything was taken care of.

My sister took a rose from the top to keep as a memory.

When we got home there were people there- and *more* food. We went outside to play, and the grown-ups brought us food to eat so we didn't have to stay inside and talk.

Some of our friends came over, and we told them about everything, and ate brownies. My friends brought a ball and we all played together.

One of my friends said they went to a funeral that wasn't a funeral.

It was a *celebration of life*, and there was no casket. Their loved one was *cremated*, and they were in a stone jar with a top on it, and their name carved into it. They went to their church for their celebration and the food was there too. They thought brownies in their own yard sounded way better.

One of my cousins said a friend of his also had someone cremated, but they *scattered their ashes* in the ocean.

Their celebration was on the boat, and they threw flowers into the sea.

Then they all went out for lunch together.

I asked what cremation meant. They said that it was when the person died their body went into a big heater that turned it from a body into ashes. The ashes can go in the jar, or the sea, or a cemetery like we went to today, or even stay at home if someone wants to keep them.

We talked about it while we kicked the ball, and one of my cousins said she wants to be cremated and to be scattered at Disneyland so all of us can go visit and be happy.

I kinda don't think that's allowed- but I like her idea. I just don't want her to die.

When everyone started leaving I helped take out lots of trash and clean up.

My dad ordered pizza for dinner. We watched a movie. I was a little worried all night.

Before I went to bed I asked my mom if she was going to die. She told me everyone does, at some time, just like our dog Maggie last year. Nobody gets to live forever here on earth. She said she was not sick, and nobody else was, and that even though we do not know exactly what is going to happen in life, she was pretty sure we would all be here for a really long time- and she hoped I would not use that time to fight with my sister, no matter how much she annoyed me. Then we read a story and it was bedtime. I was so tired.

We all had moments when we were sad for a while. My mom cried when a song played on the radio. My sister would not watch some TV shows. I felt bad that I was mad about missing my game more than sad about the person dying. My dad said that was normal, and he didn't blame me for being mad. He said next time, if there was a next time, he would make sure I got to my game.

Next week it will be a year since they died. We are going to do something that day. Some of my cousins are coming because their parents aren't planning anything. I'm hoping it will be a trip to the lake where we can play, barbecue and remember them at a place we shared.

I don't want to be sad they are dead. I want to be glad they were here. My sister wants to plant a tree at the lake so we can all watch it grow and remember them. I like that idea.

We can go back to the tree whenever we want and remember what we learned from them. I can remind my sister how much she looks like they did. My cousin can brag about throwing a ball like they did. My brother can laugh about the funny jokes they told together.

We can remember them and keep them with us.

Always.

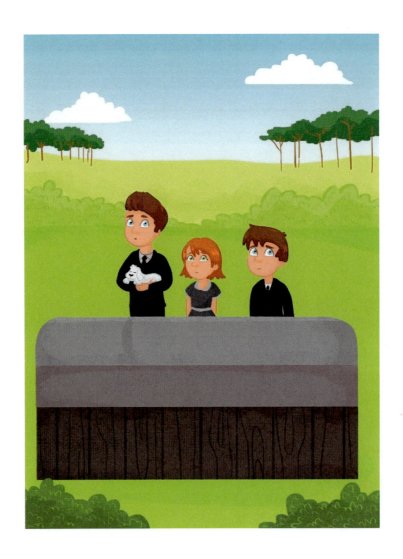

Words to know from this book:

Arrangements: All the things to be planned for a funeral or memorial service, burial or cremation. It can include flower ordering, picking out the book for people to sign, cards to be given out at the service, and planning the reception after the service.

Viewing/Visitation: A time when people can come and visit the family and the casket is present, and usually open for people to look in if they want to.

Funeral: A time where the casket is usually present when the person who died is remembered in a service, usually in a church or at the mortuary, and usually led by a minister or rabbi or other officiant. There are usually songs, and memories shared.

Cemetery: A park-like place where people are buried in caskets, and ashes are buried too. There are headstones that say who is buried where. After a funeral sometimes caskets are brought directly to the cemetery for a smaller service where the casket is left in the ground or on a stand. Sometimes funerals are held at the cemetery only.

Pallbearers: Six people who are chosen to carry the casket, sometimes at the funeral, sometimes at the cemetery.

Casket: A box that is made of metal or wood with fabric inside like a bed. The person who died is placed inside. The casket is usually buried in a cemetery.

Mortuary/Funeral Home: A place where people work to help families when someone dies. The person who died is taken there, and they put them in their casket or take them for cremation. They help with planning the services and getting everything put together for the family.

Procession: After a funeral if the casket is going to the cemetery the cars line up behind the hearse and follow each other to the cemetery.

Hearse: A special car that carries a casket.

Celebration of life: A service or get together to remember the person who died without the casket present.

Cremation: Turning a body into ashes after someone dies.

Scattering ashes: Taking the ashes somewhere special and letting them go or scattering them along the ground.

Tips for the Big People after someone dies

Children are innately curious, and *need* to know why things happen, how things happen, where things happen, and who makes them happen. If we don't fill in those blanks, their imagination will do it for them. That goes for death as well. They *need* to know. As with the birds and the bees their need is at their developmental and emotional level, and only you know what the children in your life can manage. But they need to know at least the basics.

When we do sit with them and explain what death means, and what happens after a death, we give them a sense of control when things are not "normal" for the family. That takes any fear out of the situation.

Children can be a part of a process after a death, and many want to be- they just don't know the words to say it, and they are watching the grown-ups for cues as to their emotional state. When the adults are upset, the little people are not going to want to get involved for fear of upsetting you more.

This is your chance to teach them an invaluable lesson- that death is part of life. And they can manage their emotions, and express them, and not be afraid of funerals or anything related to a death. (And you can teach them zombies are not real and do not pop out of cemeteries!) (Consider that handled.)

So here are some pointers for you, and anyone around the littles when the big people are coping after someone they love dies:

- Be honest. Always. They expect and need that from you right now.
- Use the real words: died, dead, casket, grave, sad, missing, lonely- whether it's about the emotions, or the facts, tell them what they are and use the right words.
- Explain what you have chosen for the body – burial, cremation, scattering- explain it so they know. If ashes are coming home with you, prepare them, but not so it is scary. They are ashes, not ghosts.
- Some kids respond well after a cremation to a charm with a bit of the ashes inside. Note- some don't.

- Mortuaries have a variety of ways to memorialize your loved one that are child friendly- thumb print necklaces, lockets, and more. Ask.
- Tell them you are sad (or mad, unhappy, stressed, or whatever it is at that moment). Tell them why so they associate the emotion with the event.
- Show them your tears. How else will they learn it's okay to cry when you are sad? Someone you loved died. You are supposed to be sad.
- Think of some options for them to help or participate and offer it.
- Think of things that fit their talents. Do you have a computer whiz kid? Guess who can make a video? A social butterfly? That's who can get everyone to sign the guest book or eat the cookies
- Be prepared for kids to choose, at the very last moment, to not get up and say something or play their guitar. Have a back-up plan.
- Let them wear clothes that feel good. Dress clothes are nice, but grouchy kids are not.
- Protect them from the folks you know will be too much for them. You know who I am talking about. We all have a few in our circles.
- Plan ahead for a break for kiddos. That goes for home, the mortuary, the service, the cemetery. They are, after all, kids. Yes, they need to learn the finer points of manners, hospitality and kindness. But do you need the stress of making them be perfect when you are sad, tired and wish you could go sit on a swing, too? There are always places they can go. Outside with another adult, or to a church, or temple playground, to their room for extra video game time, or to a friend's house. People want to help. Let them.
- If they want to look in a casket, allow it. If they don't, allow that.
- No kissing the dead person. Not for the littles. They may look peaceful, and nice, and asleep, but they will not feel normal.
- If there is a special relationship. Consider allowing your child to watch an adult tuck a small stuffed animal or something from them in the casket. Letters and pictures may be good for bigger kids.

- Children often respond well to helping pick out flowers, within reason. Or picking out a special flower just from them, they can bring to a service, place on the casket, or throw on the water. Again, you are including them, giving them roles they choose, and letting them have some control, within your parameters.
- Be ready for bedtime questions, and a lot of questions after a funeral.
- Talk about the person who died. Never stop. If you do, the message to them will be it is not okay to remember, or talking about them will make you too sad. Mark the special days in the calendar by including the person who died. Mark the anniversary of the death by remembering them.
- Kids need the message that it is okay to still talk to the person who died, dream about them, and share memories. The fact is kids will see the person growing up with them, and that person will play a role in their life. If you talk about them, you get to know what that role is.
- One of the best messages for kids after someone dies is, they had qualities and special things about them that will live on by remembering them, those qualities will become part of them, and in that way they will never be forgotten.
- Take care of yourself. The time after a death can be exhausting. All of you need to be kind to yourselves, rest, eat a little something good for you, and allow the emotions to happen.
- Help your children by telling them who they might look to for support.
- Allow the helpers to help. From the professionals like mortuary staff and the service officiant planning the service, to friends, family, and colleagues. Teach the children to look for helpers, to find people to talk to who are appropriate, and share what is really going on. If you model it, they will learn it.

About the author:

Jill Johnson-Young, LCSW, is a certified Grief Recovery Facilitator, Co-Founder of a successful group therapy practice in Riverside and Murrieta, California, and a therapist specializing in grief and loss, trauma, and children and families. She has decades of experience with hospice, where she specialized in pediatric care and provided children's grief groups in local schools. Jill trains therapists and social workers in areas that include correctly treating childhood trauma, grief and loss, and dementia care. She holds a BA from UC Riverside, and her MSW from the University of South Florida. Jill is the creator of Your Path Through Grief, which is a year-long, comprehensive one of a kind, grief support program. She is the author of "Your own path through grief workbook," "Someone is sick- How do I say goodbye?" and a book in development about surviving and thriving through grief. Jill is active in the dementia community and facilitates a support group in her area.

Made in the USA
Lexington, KY
22 September 2019